ADRIENNE

A POETRY JOURNAL OF QUEER WOMEN
ISSUE 02

Sibling Rivalry Press
Alexander, Arkansas
siblingrivalrypress.com

EDITOR
Valerie Wetlaufer

PUBLISHER
Bryan Borland

Cover by Ashley Inguanta. Used by permission.

All rights reserved. No part of this book can be reproduced in any form by any means without written permission. Please address inquiries to the publisher:

Sibling Rivalry Press
13913 Magnolia Glen Drive
Alexander, AR 72002
info@siblingrivalrypress.com

Printed in the United States of America.

ISBN: 978-1-937420-72-7
ISSN: 2331-9194

Adrienne: Issue 02.
April 2014.

POETRY BY

ALYSIA ANGEL ... 7

JESSICA RAE BERGAMINO ... 21

TAMIKO BEYER ... 33

SOSSITY CHIRCUZIO ... 47

CHERYL CLARKE ... 64

THERESA DAVIS ... 73

LEAH HORLICK ... 81

LAURA PASSIN ... 92

ANNE MARIE ROONEY ... 101

ARISA WHITE ... 108

ASHLEY INGUANTA ... 121

CONTRIBUTORS ... 122

ALYSIA ANGEL

Embarrassed by Our Affection

THREE ARROWS IN THE DIRT

my aunt sharon
was as bald as a coot
christmas visiting
rattling up
in her shit brown trailer
to the chagrin of
mamaw's slightly
downturned
prim rosy pink mouth
white hands fluttering
at her thick waist
like trapped birds
my aunt sharon
could wolf whistle
fix her trailer
all on her own
wiggle her non-existent brows
making her wild beehive
bouffant

half-breed cher
wig
wiggle saucily
on her smooth skull
my aunt sharon
had hands like a man
thick calloused palms
picking me up
swinging me over her head
my girl
broken picket fence teeth
bellowing laughter
in warm
ocean waves
over the knitted brows
of fine southern relatives
but never a man just a friend
the women would whisper
in the kitchen
adopted don't know her kin
flour on their backsides
my aunt sharon
was as bald as a coot
with eyes like a solar system
gentle hands
wandering heart
no need for a man's approval
for a brick home
perfect pie
pink lipstick
but always
no matter what
i was
her girl

GENIUS DAUGHTER

i taught myself to whistle
in the summer of 1977
sitting barefoot in underpants
on the motel room stoop
another gritty day gone
momma didn't care none
baby cried himself to sleep
no one but me and the neon sign

blink

blink

blinking

i could read then but
vacancy
was something felt not read
that red hot
vacancy
is what made me squint
into the frog croak of a night
pucker my lips
curl my tongue
behind my crooked bottom
baby teeth
(blow)
drooling on my dirty chin
until a faint
spit soaked
weak
little whistle
burst out of my lungs

into the sweaty
dark place
i called
home
for one night

MOHICAN MEANDERINGS

for my 16th birthday
mamaw came to visit
all the way in waco
where children who no one wanted
lived
she was uncomfortable
with me
with the outside of her house
(no iron bars to keep her safe)
pulling on her oversized purple
hand-painted tee shirt
her summer feet
like precious hooves
from the garden
after much fussing over
how i looked to her
what i needed to do for her
how much i scared her
she thrusted
a tiny silver ring into my hand
i held it in front of me
to get a good look at the thing
dainty for sure
tiny heart tiny diamond
(it's real it's real)
(with pride)
(and something else)
"well put it on, girl"
it fit perfectly size 5.5
left hand
"it was your momma's"
(looking away)
"i gave it to her on her 16th birthday"

the room became hot
smoke in the curtains
my finger began to melt
as it burned into my flesh
i turned my mouth up
stapled it into a smile
with love
"ain't it so pretty, leesha b?"
"ain't it so fine?"
(breathless)
"yes, mamaw"
the burning began to make it's way
into my throat
mamaw left quickly
embarrassed by our
affection and
one armed hug
my left arm on fire by then
flesh slowly falling off of my bone
the ring remained
debutante modesty
southern grace
(inferno)
for mamaw the ring
was a replacement
like me
like us
like my mother
the ring was
her sore hard working feet
sore heart
when i turned 36
i sold it at a pawn shop
bought myself a steak
at a restaurant i can't afford
20 years of longing and sorrow

never tasted better than
medium rare red wine glaze
chocolate cake
the moon on the walk home
to freedom

ALYSIA ANGEL

HOME IS WHERE THE SONGBIRD WAITS

while you were shaking
rogue limbs twitching
eyes like moss-lined trees
clouded by so many stranger feet
pacing scuffs
into elderly floors
our peaches were molding
i saw their ailing green bottoms
glaring at me from those shiny shelves
where you always come after my cyclone
and carefully arrange things
back in your army rows
i did nothing
because i didn't have the heart
to watch them tumble sickly
one by one
into the compost
for our spring garden
when you were sleeping
with a tube down your throat
schools of badges
swimming in my hope ocean
i sat next to a man
who loved his wife so much
that even her shit
was a medal
that he slung around his neck
he backed himself around
a compact woman who averted her eyes
her fat baby crying half heartedly
in her slack arms
while you were wheeled
down long hallways into a cool
dark cave

no older than 24
i practiced telepathy
so much
i gave myself a headache
the peaches are still
on the shelves
but i'm just going to let them rot
because when you notice them
i'll know everything
is as it should be

SHOOTING GALLERY

i found a
dead baby bird
once
pink puckered
shiny
flesh
and
half feathered
broken body
limp in my
makeshift cradle
hands
and the starlings
laughed down
from the big
oak
where i thought
fairies lived
i sat alone
cross legged
with tears plopping
on the wet ground
until papaw
found me
and
pulled me in his lap
for awhile he said nothing
me with the baby bird
and him with
everything
then
he squinted
at the sky

gravely
starlings
can't be trusted
they're
murderers
cunning
ruthless
(glorious)
he gestured at
his precious plum
trees
letting
his meaty
hand
fall back
on my shoulder
too heavy
for five
and
(softly)
some of god's creatures
are almost too cruel
to love
but we must find a way
to love them that much more
i've been watching
murmuration
videos
when they rise up
into their trusted
black knots
against screaming
blue
skies
i wonder if the
starlings
ever wish

for a
different
profession
and i know
i must
love them
that much more

FRIEND OR FERINE

in less than two years
the boys up the block
have changed
oh
they're still tangled
in a knot of open mouthed
laughing
pitching up above their heads
tumbling up the street to my window
they're still racing each other home
darkness on their heels
oh they still practice swearing
in the thicket where the prostitutes
used to make money
or take a nap
they're still the same in loud ways
that can be counted on
but something happened
as their bodies grew longer shadows
voices got grated over hot coals
they quit looking me in the eyes
around last year
when i waved at them from
the curb
their shoulders began to bow
into their chest
as if to protect
the hot heart there
their suddenly knowing
eyes
cutting
the sides of their baby fat
faces
this year they didn't scream

so joyously as they marauded
halloween style
this year they didn't offer
without solicitation
what they got for christmas
just last month i said hello
one of them mumbled
the rest stared away
fingers waving slightly
hello
or
goodbye
the boys up the street
have changed in the last
two years
back then i could have been a
distant friend
but now i am clearly
only another adult
them
not quite
men

Jessica Rae Bergamino

The Mermaid, Singing

THE MERMAID WAKES UP TO THE CLOCK TOWER'S CHIMES, TO THE FERRY'S HORNS

Docks fill with anchors, silver and constant with desire to fall.
I don't envy lead its density, nor envy bodies their ballast.

I don't envy the courage required to carry your lonely silence.

The world sings and you call it
weather.

THE MERMAID LAUGHS AT THE STORIES YOU KEEP TELLING

I would be witch and lover both,
hag and temptress,
crooked teeth with breast borne.

I would be your Eve and Lilith
cherished and chastised.

I would be your Marilyn,
your Gretel,
your Hillary,
your Ophelia,
your Mary with her skirts up.

I would be fallen,
would undo, would want
to split for two.

THE MERMAID DECLINES INTERVIEWS IN VOGUE, THE NEW YORK TIMES, AND THE ECONOMIST

Already, unwind yourself from mirage
of hose and faucet,
from steady tanks collecting Latin names.

The ways the world will be made or unmade
are more than numbers can count.

You can't undo yourself from loneliness,
it undoes itself from you.

THE MERMAID LEARNS THE MEANING OF DISTANCE

Two hemispheres, two lungs,
the bodies in orbit.
Gravity, mass, you've named them apart.

      Loneliness must feel like some great failure.

THE MERMAID LEARNS THE DIFFERENCE

One is the wing you carry inside.

Arms are bone first, muscles second,
tools third and last.

One is the wing you wear outside—
a shield about your soft body.

THE MERMAID ADDRESSES THE FOURTH GRADE CLASS WHO COMES TO VISIT HER

There are things you know someone will tell you to forget.
Small things like string and secret names.
I had an imaginary friend and held her close at night,
whispering the whole day
into her bone-locked heart.
For a long time she understood.

For a long time the world,
a cool blue rush,
will hold you from getting hooked.

THE MERMAID CONSIDERS THE PREGNANT WOMAN ON THE SHORE

Even your body becomes necessary, becomes sugar, becomes sweat. The animal unhinges your hips.

In the brightest world your words would race for breath. Hunger is always a ghost, waiting.

THE MERMAID GOSSIPS WITH THE WIND

In solitude, things cease their salt.
Even the waves want to return to shore,

want the edge between these bodies
to blur. The volume of your breath

becomes a rush of cool upon fragility
and touch is only what you make.

STUDENTS FROM THE ART ACADEMY COME TO PAINT THE MERMAID

Gulls dip and wave their fat bodies to catch your eye.
Light drips off wires into waves shrill with shadow.

Honeyed, voluminous, bright—how else to describe
the day? In countless strokes you try to court

the seen from unseen, folding and flexing against story
of necessities.
        All anyone wants is to be told what they already know.

UNABLE TO AVOID IT, THE MERMAID FEELS RAIN ON HER FACE FOR THE FIRST TIME

Bright stings as if the earth were trying to rejoin herself;
to kiss the mirror of herself;
to love herself harder and further than you.

THE MERMAID EATS

Time hums and fills your empty places
with desire. If you are good
you'll even find pleasure in survival.
If you are good.

Blue hours hum and contract inside you.
Their hooked fingers snag the hungers
you carry & the hungers to eat
what carries you.

JESSICA RAE BERGAMINO

THE MERMAID REMEMBERS SHE DOESN'T BELIEVE IN LIMITS, DECLARES HER HAPPINESS

When you walk you know where you end
because you feel the world upon you.

Wind, smoke, the sweat of steel coming down
through a city that feels its heart in the thrum

of a train beneath the ground. You spit
and it sits upon your skin,
fragrant salt.

The air is cool.
The night is warm.

Tamiko Beyer

Come Undone At Every Line

ZUIHITSU: BOSTON, APRIL 2013

Time was something that happened somewhere else to other people in other places and all I can think about is your flushed cheeks and how you cry out as we move: muscle nerve and skin.

My body a vehicle for pleasure and tremendous feeling.

What kind of terror follows pleasure.

We were less than two miles away. Bodies burned and shattered. And we keep being safe. And there is so much bad to right. And you go and go toward it.

Dearest, it's more than my body's oceanic pleasure in yours. It's the anchoring of your arms. I could be awash in undertow, the panic in someone's voice. But before I suck under you hold onto me.

When we stood at the ocean's shore level to the sea, the waves struck the rocks and water streamed over the edge in thin sheets, tiny waterfalls.

A heart holds and overflows. Cascades and returns to ocean.

The sidewalk stained with blood, a body rolling in the streets.

I buy red wine, chocolate cake. How I respond to crisis. The day is sunny and warm. I think of how we smell like salt when we lay in each other's arms.

Our country's body fills with gunpowder, palms wrapped around joysticks sending machines without bodies to slaughter, children an afterthought.

Somewhere else in time I am following my body's unruly impulse.

We are bleeding on our own sidewalks.

I am loving you vastly.

This city in which we have found ourselves. We call it home. I nestle into you, all elbows and need. You stride and stride toward what is right. I hold your sweet and tender.

It is the night after the night I know nothing while in the distance the sirens called in their emergencies.

Today, blood and bodies rolling in the streets. Today, the fierce light of women gathered in a kitchen to care for each other and right the world. Today, a red bird that sings and sings in a tree, on a wire, on a ledge, its anapestic beat. My heart, yours, ours.

SWEET TO RISE
AFTER NAN GOLDIN'S "KATHE IN THE TUB," 1984

mirror split
and your bare
image never singular
at once here
and across the city you bend
:: arm around my waist ::
twist the silvered faucet
:: hand's steady pressure to pulse ::
all the hot water rush

i'm steadying the wall's solid grid
glass :: window :: tile
but sunlight diffuses
and the litback circle flares
breasts :: nipples :: belly button
o and o and o
dearest, your cry splits
me :: mirrored and
doubled and pitched

INCLEMENT BIRTH

we broke bottles   electrified the abandoned
macadam with our rag-bone labor

smudgy fireflies in the humid night
our mouths limn the fig sweetheart

my spit polish   your steeled tongue
we gnaw   we gnaw down our scattered instinct

like the two birds banking in lusty angles
while their hatchling in its clotted nest uncoils   wet from shell
        beak   a widening raw

AND THUS A PROPORTIONAL RELATIONSHIP BETWEEN THEM

Your red dress was a quality I could not predict.
My red dress was of equal proportions.
Our wills matched like magnetic fields—
equal parts attraction and repellence.

In the middle, a tiny song of respite.
Before you fought for more, after,
for stasis if not equilibrium. Swing or entropy.
The syntax of our speaking together created

a form of music popular before the advent of digital technology.
Once, I had a thought about loving you,
but it turned out to be a vector on the negative x axis.
You said it is easier to stay in the past with each other

—no matter how horrible—than to confront
an unknown future apart. I am an optimist, I disagree.
Still, there is the way we find ourselves like sticky
liquor residue inside a tumbler the morning after.

(We always drank too much.) Parallel lines will never
meet up, not even in infinity. And that, finally,
is how we are. I will wave to you as we pass through
the spectrum through which colors filter.

This is a form of apology like an unbalanced equation.

GRIEF'S MECHANICS ARE NEVER WELL OILED

The wind blows
grit in the gears.

~~

I cut
a pear, leave half
face down
in the glazed bowl
to keep cool
until she wakes.

~~

Once a body grew
so close
to another body—
vines choked
both windpipes.

~~

The twitchy day
will have none of it.
Its layered sky
tosses birds
all chaos, no rest.

TOWARD SOLSTICE

binding :: small tongue
pressed to page

winter filled with winter
fruit :: curved

line :: language
stitched into body's

other meaning
light :: late

and clear :: a year's
labor pinned

THIS POEM FIRST APPEARED IN THE ASIAN AMERICAN WRITERS WORKSHOP'S THE MARGINS, JAN. 2014.

GRIEF BECOME BONE

and in a somehow place
a love you say a beating
mean a heart in earnest

what we do to breathe
rub the thin glass edge until it sings
and one of us reaches

a hand up to the ceiling
                    :: no ::
sky where grey clouds hang
soft as a paper note creased

upon itself again to cottony fibers
where your finger pressed
hard against the fold

as if sustained pressure
could make the words inside
take on muscle and somehow it did

a body then two
then a dozen accounted
for all of us folding

upon ourselves relentless waves
return to rock face
all of us back to a gesture like bowing

if the last one standing
smile a little crooked
but the right bit

of tenderness and the right
amount of power
in our arms exactly enough

to palm
the sky
then all of us release

SUBTERRANEAN HAIBUNS

1
Night's pale passage / cast across floor's thin bones / into the deep.

To sleep is to fall into something like another universe. In that other universe I have a different string of lovers. The three-legged pig is not a pig but a bird. The bird is a folk story that gives us strength. The problem with symbols: they carry too much weight. Or, they are simply tokens. I have come so close to being scarred by symbols. The why behind the sacred. Some secrets are best kept secret. Once we open our mouths, toads and jewels spill out. In the fairy tale, someone spews a mouthful of precious gems, another spews a species of frogs. Imagine carrying all that hardware in your stomach. Days of due diligence, kicked in your belly and it's not even a baby; it's a creature. When I was born, the cicadas chirped to themselves, a desperate situation. The air hung heavy across our skins. There were not many others in the room. My mother and my father and a person to help bring me into the world. I as I was not planned for, despite their desire to create a being.

2
Dream a walk with you / along the rusting shoreline / the moon's bare candor.

Because we are always arriving with new yeses at the ocean's shore. Because there are great white sharks out in the waters, because human flesh is still soft and vulnerable and delicious. Because what is delicious is forbidden. Because being forbidden, the skin is even more desirable. Because desire is a mountain and a lake. Because the body, always, because it begins and ends with the body. Because what has happened for thirty-eight years will continue happening. Because of heat. Because it keeps us safe, because of the sun. Because of dirt and because of water. Because we come at the problem from one way and then another. Because nothing is more impossible than pure song. Because song is a metaphor for want. Because ideas continue to push forward even when bodies are no longer. Because the mind cannot truly be separated from the flesh. Because we try all the same. Because trying makes it so, to a certain extent. Because there's the subterranean, where temperatures are cooler and memories are sharper. Because a time of incubation. Because grief. Because what it means to lose an entire human being. Because the soul is a concept of all or nothing. Because if you didn't grow up believing in god, what do you have. Because if you grew up among the silk crates of religion, and then leave it behind, what do you have. Because all of childhood is about finding the mystery of existence. Because where are the answers.

3
Now another you—/ horizon line silver and full / tide's swift basin.

Systems say go. It's not sleep I'm looking for, it's an all-around digging. The cicadas are as loud as engines and the clock on the wall is a moment-to-moment demonstration of how time moves. The ritual unfolding. *God*—that concept I lost track of long ago. Not so, conquest. A country of beaches, white sand, a waterfall, a lake filled with carp. How we take over and never let go. The blue sky and the blue necktie. It was hot, my body incubated. The fish was raw and cold. I would not be the kind of woman who goes ahead without first asking about precedent and political viability. Bubbles, bubbles. The way light hit the water, the way water carried us forward. One can go out closed and then come back smooth sailing. The physical wave of the ocean, how it sucks from below, crashes against the sky, gives us back our stripped bones. My body undergoing lessons in loss. Jewels and frogs, what it no longer needs to hold. The way I throw a pebble clear across the day to land in your lap. Today it was your fingers I was noticing. How long they are, rimmed by tiny white moons.

4.
You said apricot / I thought you said ritual. / I wanted to taste.

Friend, the cicadas are full throating their summer swan song. I know the days will grow shorter and colder: the first leaves have already fallen. When I look into the trees, the sparks there in June are no longer: pulsing light across the leaves' veins. By August, life is already burrowing into the roots to stay underground until spring's speed through capillaries, the burst again into unfurling. The days will grow cold and that is how the year curls onto itself. But for now, it is high summer and I am to give you an anaphora, a repetition across lines, a talisman. I said that symbols are only tokens but I don't think I believe it. What is good luck is what has come into our lives with astonishing speed and surety. This is how I say to you that everything will be fine, because the cicadas are going full throttle ahead, and what the insects know, if they know anything at all, is the sheer force of life and their insistence of song, despite their hard, shelled lives. I have come with pen and paper to record the journey of twelve children, or the light that has come to stand for children. Sometimes we have only the silver, the hard tines of a fork. Love, the cicadas buzz into themselves, high summer, their swan song; they will soon be silent and translucent. The shades of color across the evening sky telling us what we need to know.

5
Our superhero / braver than her childhood allows / sings herself to sleep.

When I was born there might have been a thunderstorm. But that is the story of someone else's birth. I have shown a predilection for stealing; now might be the time to stand guard. Back to my birth. It was the 1970s. Nixon had just resigned. People lined up for gas. A summer full of strange days. I was a child born into grainy circumstances. The summer became something more than beautiful when my mother pulled back her hair to feed me. Still, powerful men continue to lie. Tonight the rock band Pussy Riot is in jail for spitting their bodies and voices across pews, pissing off a powerful man. Not god. When I was 17 someone spray painted *riotgrrrrl* across the side of the high school. Red dripped down stucco and of course I held up my fist, and then I bit down hard. I did not know I was to enter a life of summer dresses and heels, all deviant. A teenager coming into my body, learning its lit language.

6.

A lagoon and vegetation / dogs pull at their leashes / green grows into ground.

Into the deep and the trees sweeping across the rooted levels of government. We had no more real places to stay, but we did it anyway, hat in hand and motorcycle between our legs. Too many times I have gone the other way: into the magnificent trailer of dirt and desire. I was dreaming of something that looked like roses, but the worms and iron windows prevented us from going as underground as we need. Your scarred neck. That's where our confessions lie. And then we come out swinging because we have done nothing wrong. We come out swinging because wilderness merits a kind of danger. I have always been kin to wolves, and this is a howling that is against bricks and deception. A howl of funerals. I say how many rituals have we lost. There are certain moments when I know giving up is not the way to get to reckoning, but I do it anyway. When I need to see things anew. You said beautiful must be broken to remain beautiful, quoting a woman who broke, in the end, unable to live a bodied life, unable to burrow down as much as she needed to survive. And you, gorgeous mosaic of fragments, loss and survival. As for me, impossible to live in a body not set trembling like a cello's string. What I'm saying: we attend the world's every move and come undone at every line.

THIS POEM FIRST APPEARED IN VOLTA, ISSUE 24, DEC 2012

Sossity Chiricuzio

Places of Deepest Joy

SALTED CARAMEL

what are these places
of deepest joy?
some small object
scent, or touch
wiring directly into a childbodymemory
imprinted so far beneath conscious thought
the moment of remembering is a flashflood
washing every other brain channel clear
in colors vivid beyond the wavelength
of any cone cell i now own
details and emotion
deep cave selenite sharp-edged clear
for a timeless time
that is not time enough
and then
bittersweet and fading
like the last lick of salted caramel
on the back of your teeth
and the wondering

what set it so strong, there?
waiting
quiet
behind a dam
i don't remember building
overabundance of memories
layering watertight over the years?
the price of growing up, by which i mean into
the roles the world, and adult, requires
by which i mean
childhood knowledge
clarity
goes misty
like a photo behind glass
left in the sun
through a window
in a shed's back wall
at the top of a half open box
with no label
forgotten
fading
until the photochemical reaction
throws a sharp contrast
and there
that vivid moment
flows rich over every sense
rare
those moments
but they strike a note
so resonant
that i can feel my child
self
like an anchor
and also
a kite

OUTLAW

your tipped fedora smile
and bourbon-spiked voice
drive my '46 mercury body
around every curve of this road
foot relaxed over the pedals
hands easy on the wheel
no way to know if you'll
put on the brakes
or speed us up and over the hill
it's a delicious not-knowing
that makes my smile so wide
it reflects this blue moon
while my hair blows
in the soft wind
of your satisfied chuckle
it is a creation myth
it is a fairy tale
it is improv theater
comedy
open mic
confession

it is the longing of atoms
and a primate's dream
it is heady gender
tender feelings
life worn flesh
trusting
and flying
or falling
as the lesson requires
it is old family dynamics
and new disappointments

it is art, heart and soul
it is bone, blood and philosophy
it is oxygen
it is prayer

you clasp my fingers
put them into your mouth
taste the musk and hope
I left there for you
you show me your scar
that leads to desire
you teach me the rhythm
that finds your glory
you sing me your song
I don't know the words
but my hum satisfies
and I learn with repetition

we roll to a gentle stop
stretch our legs
catch our breath
then come together
iron to magnet
a joyous collision

I let you see my shadow
the one that shows in the dark
the one that lights the path
if you find it
put your hand over my heart
twist, just so
and release
if you listen
it will open
pour out my
divine beast

my
fearsome
gentle
knowledge
all the characters
that can hold my
spirit
and hunger
the tapestry
of self
that I would share

let you
finger my knots

tangle yourself
in my unraveled edges

braid a rope to bind me
down
to
set me free
to
hold back my hair
while you kiss your way
along the nape of my neck
over my shoulder
to that spot where your teeth
bring submission
a pleasure akin
to gazing at the sun
for just a second
dazzled and
boundless

no ground
no sky
simply skin
and what is against it
your weight
pressing me into the dirt
your entrance
like lightning
striking
the same place twice

bonfire
brushfire
conflagration
of cool waves
washing me
sacred
I am, you are
we are
sanctified
outlaw

THIS POEM ORIGINALLY APPEARED ON THE CD HAND TO MOUTH.

LEARNING CURVE

this is my fat body
in your bed

this is my fat body
naked
in your bed

this is my fat body
naked
open
vulnerable
on fire
lusted after
in your bed

this is not
an accident

not settling

not for my
pretty face

my kind
and generous
heart

this body
is great
at fucking

loves to fuck
your body

it's in my
pheromones
and my sly
smile

letting you

look at me

drink your fill

until your eyes
overflow
and i'll lick that
salt
too

this body
cradles
envelops
slaps back
into your hand
shameless

this body
spreads
flows
exposes core
swallows your hand
joyous

this was all
hard won

this body

was invaded
was pilfered
was weighed and found
wanting

rude eyes
words crude

i fought my way
tooth
nail
politics
tears
faith

back
into this body
all the way up to the skin
from 3 spans
back

i re-associated
myself
with the feel of it
heft
scents
tastes
sounds
movement

a learning curve
still curving

so when i say
this body

what i mean is
my body

my bones
nerves
organs
muscle
fat
skin
fur

my folds
rolls
mounds
rises
dips
inner
outer

this is my fat body
in your bed

this is my fat body
naked
in your bed

this is my fat body
naked
scared
imperfect
trusting
healing
in your bed

loves to love
this is not
an accident

there's safety

in your
informed desire

your kind
and generous
heart

you're great
at fucking
my body

seeing
craving
thorough
honest

licking my
salt

drinking your
fill

DRUNK ON DESIRE

drunk on desire
and the multiplication
of joy
your fingers
her cock
someone's mouth
my skin is yearning
upward
outward
trying to make more surface area
for every surprise
touch
feather light
raking nails
solid blow
my compass is spinning
only the feel
of my back
pressed into the bed
belies the feeling
of levitation
a slap to the face
reminds me to breathe
the air races in
and in
a rush
i feel in my toes
curling
into the sheets
seeking an anchor

merciless
tender
you gather
to feast

my eyes
sequestered
fill in the blanks
with sparks of light
deep red violet
at the sink of teeth
into shoulder
merging with
hot white flash
of leather's edge
and her sweet
dirty
whisper
trails pink tendrils
down my neck
they run together
crimson hot
melting
between my thighs
a palate
varied
as the artist's
canvas
landscape
you travel
fearless

safe
in the chaos
of wild natures

set free
raucous
loving
cruel
as any
gatekeeper
to truth
challenging
the depth of hunger
the determination
to know self
to be known
seen
naked to the bone
beyond voice

a circle
of arms
welcoming
me home

BODIES DON'T PLAY FAIR

this pain of mine
it scares you
due to no lack of courage
on your part
or mine
unsure
how to balance
what my body won't
and what yours will
how to freely dance
even when i have to
sit this one out
how to
help
i know
your tender heart
aches
when my bones
ache
becomes visible
on my face
in my stride
you want to
help
want to
fix
want to
save
and this is life
sometimes
you can't save
or fix
but you help

you park close
walk slower
track those
broken sidewalks
and shadows
hand on my elbow
right by my side
cuddle up on the shoulder
not sore
offer to switch sides
carry my bag
run errands
without ever
diminishing my strength
you don't question
my self knowledge
but care enough to ask
the hard questions
you let me cry
without cringing away
from pain
that isn't yours
or yours to fix
you are my hero
when called on
without ever making me
small
weak
pitiful
you revel in the moments
i can scoop you up
sweet boy in my
strong femme arms
never doubting
or fearing a fall

you pin me down
for all the reasons
we both love it
rough and tumble
without too much pressure
on joints
or my sense of pride
in being burly
you win
fair
when you win
both of us smiling
either way
both of us fully
embodied
even when
bodies
don't play
fair

Cheryl Clarke

Resistance for Us

MAY DAY
EXCERPT FROM "MEDITATIONS ON WASHINGTON, D.C."

Should we celebrate the fall
of the Berlin Wall
or mourn the failures of democracy?

To think Marian Anderson may be more remembered for singing to 75,000 people in front of the 'Great Emancipator's' sculpture in Jim Crow D.C. after being refused Constitution Hall by the D.A.R. instead of for that stunning voice—at turns deep, clear, muddy, atonal, bell-like almost flat sometimes with the crystal longing of 'Deep River,'
and the loneliness
of separate dining.

RACING TERROR
FOR KATRINA SURVIVORS

i. high dive

i'm glad my mother died two years before this mess or she mighta
    been one of those old old women trapped by the water as it
    swole up to the
3rd
4th
5th floor
& she couldn't git out & drown-ded remembering her salad days
    on the high dive.
as it was she died of congestive heart failure, a drowning of another
    sort.
she went down hard, cursing us all for not rescuing her
from the end.
damn—katrina! damn katrina? damn, katrina.

ii. new deal

roosevelt's way to deal with the dixiecrats and jim crow.
huac.
federal fair employment practices.
truman integrates the army.
mccarran.
mccarthy.
martyrdom of malcolm x.
murder of martin king:
    memphis, oh, memphis.

COINTELPRO.

1973:
blood and

BLA stencils dot a trail along the n.j. turnpike
up to welfare reform.
patriot act.
levees breeched.

iii. 'only whites need relocate to mississippi'

'brownie' called you all day long to tell you the category 5 was gonna
    wash the crescent away.

won't listen. can't listen. don't wanna listen. nothing and nothing
    will stop oil rich dixiecrat
Texans who won't relocate to oil-rich nigeria
and nagin
crying from a holiday inn.

'only whites need relocate to mississisppi (or washington, d.c.).'

iv. 'there ain' no place fo' a po' ol' gal to go'

nobody cares what happens to niggers, especially poor ones, like those ones with nappy hair and bad cholesterol cursing the government from the superdome.
(the ones—so unlike oprah winfrey—whose feet barbara bush do not want on her coffee table nor do oprah. but they hurt 'like nobody's business.').
we knew them before katrina.
just like those iraqi so-called insurgents creeped up into the middle
    of the wmd lies.
katrina busted those levees. lies. levees.
prescription/prescripting drug fiascos.

'what?! what?! medicaid does not cover my diabetes medicines no more! well, scarlet, you can just pull that $200 out yo' ass. i'm gon' go buy me some smack cook it up and git some use outta these syringes and git it all ovah with before that bird flu git here.

no quarantine for me. terrorists take me to hell.'

v. delaware county to the parish of orleans

   a thousand miles north
   we pass a beauteous cemetery:
   stones old as 1803
   diminutive stones for:

   2 3 4 5 6

children
dead at 10 weeks to 13 years.
   the great blue heron lands on a marshy field
     and takes off immediately arcing its neck.
      we follow the sound of its wings
        under a 21 foot high
        wall of water.
      to other graves above-
    ground then to ramparts street
  alighting
 atop
a mule-drawn funeral pyre

a runaway and an orph
an girl walk shoulder to sh
oulder to claim and rename
   congo square.

URBAN EPITAPHS, POST 9/11

i. Kyra Mills
(posted with photo on a mailbox at 14th St. and 6th Ave., New York City, N.Y., fall 2001)

6 years old
last seen hold-
ing her mother's hand on the 92nd floor of Tower One.

ii. Chopra Dias
(posted with photo at the Newport PATH Station, Jersey City, N.J., fall 2001)

works on the 107th floor.
Last seen: 9/11
is diabetic
and wearing college ring on left hand.

iii. not the only
9/11:

Chile. 1971. CIA coup d'état.
Suicide. Murder. Rape.
Arena of torture.
Unnamed women and girls.

Survivors of Pinochet
clanging pots and pans
to shame his atrocities.
Never enough clanging.
Never enough shaming.

CHERYL CLARKE

ANTIQUARIAN BOOKSELLER
FOR DIANA

You kept your word and the discount prevailed for this
first edition Harlem Shadows at fifty dollars; but
would McKay think it a fair fee for this antique volume
      of early but famous verse (which didn't much improve)
      and $1.75 in 1922 hardcover 18 years
before pocket books' invasion and me a sucker lover of
      hardcover New Negro efforts and worth
throwing itself at the feet of Europe and so forth as Eastman
      takes me aback anew raving
universality despite white people's failure still

to imagine themselves slaves.

Yes, this McKay my bookshelf craves—
more than its previous owner's—'Mary Jo Lamb'
of the pretty hand, as precious as this first edition.

IN THIS HOSTILE CORRIDOR

A quickening nostalgia suffuses
me, this late evening fin de siècle
between two endangered sites.
The marvelous have been blighted
by a blood-borne scourge. Flam-
boyantly frail, pretty,
still marvelous you nourish my failing
geographies. As I face your soliticitousness
over the counter of this nasty KFC
and am dazzled by your articulated brows,
mascara, the discrete texture
of your facial skin, and cultivated nails,
you recognize me too—
by my precise haircut.

PREVIOUSLY PUBLISHED AS PART OF A LONGER WORK IN CHERYL CLARKE, THE DAYS OF GOOD LOOKS, PROSE AND POETRY 1980-2005.

THE (ONLY) ATHLETE
EXCERPT FROM "BLACK MEN (ALWAYS IN PROGRESS)"

    Jack
         Roosevelt
Robinson,'Jackie,'
1947, integrated white
baseball a portion of the game
devoted to controlling   himself:
grandson of a slave the Negro   Leagues
overqualified Branch an experiment: insults,
  loneliness, and abuse 'hey boy, come pick
    my cotton.' tensions high   and Rachel
     in the stands rooting   (Rachel al
       ways rooting) Pee Wee 29 stolen
            bases the death of the   Ne
            gro Leagues   star of
                    his own bio pic.
         Ja
ck

    ie

C a m p a i g n i n g
for Nixon in 1960.
Derided by Malcolm
X as a 'Tom.'
The death of
J a c k i e J r.
Did he really do
more for the Negro
than Martin Luther
King Jr.? Did Malcolm X
really read *Uncle Tom's Cabin*?

CHERYL CLARKE

MY BROTHER NEEDS AT LEAST

a poem
queer small swimmer painter pianist
coulda been a winner
in another time
another father or
a mother who had later been acquitted of homicide
and still later remarried
(my mother too)
expected you to get a job in the gov't
whatever else you did with
your excessive gifts.
you chose air force. error.
discharged and trained as a draftsman. dried your soul.
29 years at the pentagon. (witnessed the loss to fire of the 'secret
    data.') not a day without vodka.
dead from its ravages
queer small swimmer painter pianist
with your military so-long-salute somewhere in Virginia.
your butch colleague
her uncomfortable skirt and shoes
a heart-wrenching eulogy.
Two of your sisters also eulogized. The
other two of us suppressed our funereal corniness.
Mother hid her blindness behind her customary glamor.
For the second time in my life, I met your daughter, painter and
    singer, dying of Lupus, holding your flag to her breast.
    her own daughter shipping to Afghanistan this August.

Yes, you my brother need at least
a poem.

Theresa Davis

Love Me in Daytime

BEFORE YOU DREAM OF ME TONIGHT

Before you dream of me tonight, you must first know,
that the strongest muscle in proportion to its size
in the human body is the tongue. I held my tongue once
in the roof of my mouth for almost a decade, now I appreciate its
      power.

A person cannot taste food unless it is mixed with saliva.
Every time I see you my mouth dries up desert. I haven't
had a tasty meal in months.

Your stomach has to produce a new layer of mucus every two weeks
otherwise it will digest itself, and thirty-five percent of the people who
use personal ads for dating are already married. My biological father
used to take me on dates with the women he cheated on my mother with,
and I have tried to find someone not you, but I do not trust the process.
I have seen what cheating does. I want no part of it.

Did you know a duck's quack doesn't echo, and no one knows why?
I have screamed to the sky in nightmares and no one stirred.

Maybe in my dream I was a teal, waters churning, if I drowned
who would know? Those times I woke heart pounding.

Banging your head against a wall uses 150 calories an hour.
I've been losing weight steadily these past months and
I have a little headache.

If you yelled for 8 years, 7 months, and 6 days,
you would have produced enough sound energy
to heat one cup of coffee. I start the day with at least two cups.
For you I might consider switching to tea.

Butterflies taste with their feet. If I could forget the sound
of my dad no longer breathing maybe my hands wouldn't
shake so much. You once asked about my rings.
I wear them to control the tremors.

Bullet proof vests, fire escapes, windshield wipers,
and laser printers were all invented by women.
I have this scar on my forehead. I don't remember the impact
or the passing out just waking with blood in my eyes.

Honey is the only food that doesn't spoil
and most lipstick contains fish scales.
The first time I kissed you, that night
I dreamed oceans and mermaids.

FLIGHT 69

The TSA likes to touch me. She likes to touch me in special places.
She likes to touch me like a lover. Do you love me?
The TSA likes her hands in my hair, thinks I'm hiding things in there.
She thinks I am missile launch.

The TSA likes to remind me that I can opt out and yet, she often reminds
        me
that I cannot opt out. She likes my curves, my dangle, and my sighs of
        pleasure.
She likes my first date, second, third base. She likes my moans,
my call-me-later breathy. She thinks we are dating and well, maybe.

The TSA likes my lotion and my vibrator together, wants to know
if we can get together. She sees me coming, applies lip gloss and lube
knows how I like it firm and rough. Her protected hands play over my
        body.
She thinks I am music. The TSA thinks we are going steady, well,
        maybe.

The TSA wants to have my babies and I wonder, if she is part unicorn
so we can do the damn deed already then I can stop feeling cheap.
The TSA and I will have babies that shit glitter.
The TSA will want to marry me, well, maybe.
The TSA will want a pre-nup.
The TSA will be disappointed.

The TSA dressed up for me today. Sent me a proper lesbian
and when she pats me down she feels me up. She is feeling me up
and she is the right build, and type, and she gives me her number.

The TSA will get a call tonight, and I hope she brings those
really attractive blue gloves.

TRUE ART

when you unsheathe your tongue
check the blade
the prickle sharp
make sure the handle fits your grip
so the splitting and slicing brings
you the maximum amount of pleasure
choose scythe or sickle
rip razor or machete
the type of blade is important
you want your lacerations clearly defined
want to make sure it penetrates
the intersection of your lie and the liar you've become
you want to make sure that the nick nip notch
of your scandalous revisionist history
hits the targeted audience
you want to change the pronouns
to assure you have a proper
closed closet burial

when I turn my back remind yourself
that it's not disrespect and you have no accountability here
you just got caught up in your own game
and I am just collateral damage
friendly fire but sharper
an unveiling canvas arms splayed like on an easel
and when you stab use both hands
make sure you catch the groove in my spine
make it count
bury it to the hilt
make it steamy steel magic
make me a monster you have to slay to save yourself
cum dripping off my tongue
make me pornographic larger than life

the biggest dick in the yard
make sure you jiggle it around in there
get it really messy
make sure you hit bone
Jackson Pollock me
then hold on tight

SUICIDAL TENDENCIES

At my worst I am a kamikaze lover, reckless in my falling.
Two months grounded, you enter the house through a door not a
    window.
Wrapping my sex around your fingers, men are much too easy.
I can never come back to you, this bridge has to burn.

Two months grounded, you enter the house through a door not a
    window.
Night-light and late love leave marks that cannot be seen in day.
I can never come back to you, this bridge has to burn.
Maybe one day you will love me in daytime.

Night-light and late love leave marks that cannot be seen in day.
Wrapping my sex around your fingers, men are much too easy.
Maybe one day you will love me in daytime.
At my worst I am a kamikaze lover, reckless in my falling.

THURSDAY

I am two weeks overdue. This house with no windows or doors.
My occupant, tired and drawn like blinds. The last time she spoke,
she was wind chime whisper, faulty wiring and not today.
She drug her bones, they clattered broken speech.
She was a reflection of what she used to be.
She vanished whenever she spoke.
Then suddenly one day, she became rage and rancor.
Syllables spilling from her every one laced with lonely regret.
She vanished right inside of me. This house could no longer
feel her and that was on Thursday.

On Thursday, the laundry would not dry and the pillow
rejected the weight of her hair. She left the lights on
used up all the power. This house was cold and dark
as she specter-ed herself haunting my hallways.
She left her secrets everywhere, now everyone knows.
She promised she'd return. She promised for real this time
She would keep her riotous tongue in her pocket.
That was on Thursday.

It is Sunday now, and she has not stepped foot in a church
for decades, so this house knows she is not praising God
or singing with her good voice. She does those things in private.
This house has a room full of evidence. She is hidden away now
but she promised she'd return. She hasn't been seen in days.
These walls no longer hold the fragrance of her.
Her shadows have faded from my face.
And I fear, this house fears, she is indecision and missing in
    action.
A leafless tree swaying near to falling. She is gone.

It is Thursday again. My windows, my door have not returned.
I am a house: no arms, or fingers, no voice, so I cannot tell anyone

that she has not returned. I cannot beg for them to keep looking.
This house has no foundation. She, this house, is shaky, lone and
        lonely
everywhere. Sometimes this house hears voices in the attic of her
        memories,
wonders if they might be her own. Wonders if she puts the
        voices in her mouth
will she recognize the language, feel her tongue again?
Will she know herself if she does?
She is gone, she is this house. And this house wonders.

Is it Thursday again.

Leah Horlick

You Can Tell Just by Watching Her

THE CIRCUS

        All those nights camped out in the field, squinting
for a light, a flicker, calliope in the grass.
        Grease and fire, they'd understand
and tuck you into their silken fold. They'd fawn
        and dress you, glitter and eventually parade.
You bought your ticket, held your flag at the front
        of the empty line, shut your eyes.
If you counted to one hundred, they'd appear.
        Every ninety-nine you opened up to silence.
The field was set on fire and still you stood, wedded
        to your acrobats, the promise of trapeze and escape
artists, soon. Your body changed and bled and the year came
        when you knew you would die on the highway,
in a truck bed, in a grain silo, tied to a fence, in a slough,
        at your own small hand. You left to find them.

GHOST HOUSE

Because you are broken she moves you
        into the house of cracked things—

faucets, aquariums, lamps on
        the nightstand, then off again.

Because you will never be enough she moves
        you into the house of what she can measure—

water heaters, electrical meters, thermostat
        and ticking dial.

And because you are of a kind, the house knows
        you. When you cry out,

the lights flicker, ghostly blue and ragged.
        When she says you are *shut off,*

the light switches nod their white tiny
        heads. Tiles creak *yes* beneath her

edicts—*something bad must have happened*
        to make you this way, the way

where you don't want her. But the windows
        rattle and disagree. In their honeyed,

blindless light, they see it—something bad
        is *happening.*

THE DISAPPEARING WOMAN

With her new magic, she makes you
        invisible.

The women with black eyes
        do not see you, in your bare

sleeves, your tired, unmarked face.
        The women with black eyes

can say *doorknob*. Can say *staircase*
        and *fell down*.

She doesn't give you black eyes, and
        the doctors do not see her, not in your

long hair, your good earrings, in your quiet
        descriptions of pain. They would say

boyfriend. They would see *husband*. She
        does not give you black eyes,

she is not your husband, and you do not
        say anything.

SUIT OF FEATHERS

1. Peregrine

You are trying to decide if you will go with her, for good, this time
    through the morning-dark grid of semis and orange lights,

oil fires and freight yards. Like most, you came here first
    to drink on the cusp of eighteen. Dressed in black,

fed gin and grenadine at the goth bar, you listened to industrial,
    the signs
    that told you not to snort coke in the bathroom. No one
    listens

to those signs in Alberta, now. With all that rolled-up money the
    city courts
    her. You drive the long stretch and count the rigs

drilling their beaks into the fields, come up with reasons,
    and throw them back to the ground again.

2. Chickenhawk

In the single room you rent because it's cheaper,
        where no one will know you're a couple, where

you sneak her bags up the back stairs, she tells you
        we could live here. It's legal in Alberta—

stripping. She knows you've thought about it.
        Some women, *you can tell just by watching them.*

You can pay off my student loan.
        When you ask her if she knows

what the definition of a pimp is,
        like in that one Michelle Tea poem,

where all her friends want her to trick
        so they can go for smoothies again,

she rolls into the wall and won't talk.
        She hasn't read the poem.

There's no word for this woman. Not madam, cougar
        or chickenhawk. You can tell just by watching her.

3. Raven

In the morgue for birds at the university
        of Alberta, the smell of freezer-burn

and blood, feathers, and the way she touches them
        turns you. Sceptre of a frozen eagle.

Silver cabinet full of falcons. You don't ask
        to see the raven, only imagine the shelter

of its frostbitten wingspan. You stand in the hall,
        elbows tight against your ribs,

watch coils of steam circle her feet,
        the hands and talons. She calculates

the speed of a T.rex from the ancient bones
        of new creatures. Nothing is wasted.

The birds are safe here, flightless,
        sharp and cold, kept from rotting.

If you move here, for her, she tells you
        to write your will, common law.

Asked what you would leave to her,
        you look at the birds, and think, *nothing.*

4. Buzzard

You knew it was bad. But not like this.
        Late afternoon walk down Whyte and already they're at
            you.

The man as big as you both side-by-each and day drunk
        blocks your path—*Can I ask you a question?*

No, you tell him, push past. You can feel the fear
        molting from her like feathers. It's your fault.

You're the confirmation, your long hair, those shoes
        beside her. Outside the good restaurant

with the sidewalk line-up, outdoor patio, west-facing
        windows to catch the oil money, the sunset

a man sticks his tongue between
        two fingers and calls you for what you are.

Yes. You wheel and turn, *make a scene*. You are not
        scared anymore, until you look ahead

and see her shouldering away from you,
        head down, through the crowd.

5. Sparrow

You find her at the entrance to that antique shop
        you both liked. Where you buy the white mugs

with the koi fish, blue scales feathered into china.
        This is not the first time she will tell you

to be quiet. *You made us look*
        just as bad as he did.

6. Vulture

In the cards you hide from her under the bed,
        you keep drawing seven feathers.

A scene of two birds at feast
        on another, nearby train tracks,

the bones not yet clean. And then that stray
        other vulture, circling in the corner—

shadow-and-feathered part of yourself, wheeling
        over trains while you are picked apart

by your own kind. Someone needs to be the witness,
        unable to look away from the wreck.

LEAH HORLICK

FOR YOUR OWN GOOD

The cats are a test.
First, you have to catch them—brown
and grey flashes in the barn, soft-pawed
and pouncing across sawdust.
Left alone with her mother,
you bring two handfuls of kitten to the raw
table. They squirm and curl against
your sweater. You can't yet grab creatures
by the back of the neck the way
she taught you to—

*It's fine! They learn this
from their mothers!*

You still flinch. You're afraid of being
scratched, or worse and what else
lives in this barn—owls, mice,
even her mother. And when
the horses come in at night.

*We're going to vaccinate the kittens
down at the barn.* You've practiced saying it
all day, worked yourself up. If you try
you can almost drawl.
Her mother brings out the long needle,
speaks to you in a voice so quiet you know
it's for the cats. Your job is to hold them.
Her mother's hands are red

and steady. She finds a loose nook of fur,
presses the syringe down, kittens
purring the whole time. *See? Easy.*
Years from now, you think of her,

by the back of her neck, gripped and screamed.
Every false punishment. That fear—

what you learn from your mothers
about helplessness,
and each other.

Laura Passin

Things She's Forgotten

OCTOBER

Fireplace, window:
one tree burns to ash
and lights this night;
another flames to brilliance outside,
though in the dark we cannot see
its violent reds.

I reach to the heat's shimmer
and my skin glows fallout orange,
obscene as aftermath, except
for one knuckle's scar, barely visible,
stark line white
and dim against the light.

You laughed at that scar,
how clumsy I'd been:
knife-slip from a cardboard box.
My hand pulsed
for days, a second heart

in the bone.
Once I loved how you spoke
the words into my body, called
hipbone from flesh,
gave the white chaos
of my back your name.
Fire fed by your breath,

my whole skin become tongue.
When you cut me from you,
I healed around your voice,
so that even the skin
surrounding this scar
flares with your memory.

Its guttered inch marks time
as the leaves on the standing tree
name the season:
surfaces die gorgeously,
leaving the thick stalk
to last through another fall.

You've slipped from the riot of my skin
to the history of my body—
like this scar that refuses
to burn, these trees that don't let go
without giving up
their most luminous colors.

FOR ANNA

You might be doing it right now: a push,
another, and again, and then, your son,
a tiny wreck of mucus, blood, a squashed
and bleary face, as though the thought of sun
and air were too exhausting to be borne.
But thought itself does not exist for him,
not yet, unless it counts as thought to mourn
the only place he knows, the quiet, dim,
and terrifying inside. Bodies don't
unlock for everyone; they keep secret
the chemistry that runs us, they don't want
the doctor's hand. This boy's another not
to ask: he swam, and now he breathes. The world
you gave him pulses as his fist unfurls.

AGAINST FIRST LOVES

Suppose the girl who left
instead became the girl you married,

suppose the times had changed,
the laws had passed,

so you got the rings, the dresses,
changed the names.

You marched on capitals, side by side,
your kiss on courthouse steps

flashed across the evening news.
You have too many cats and nieces.

Suppose she never pushed you away.
Suppose your skin never shattered like glass

in slow motion, the cracks tracing themselves
before the whole sheet collapsed.

Suppose the you that tore and healed
and aged and forgave is just a possible

woman who never chanced to exist:
a homunculus, an aborted thing.

Suppose you were happy to be rid of her.
Suppose that happiness made you whole.

INVOCATION

My fingers dream people I will never meet,
fugitive thumb-pulses,
slender uncurved toes,
strangers' veins.

In their place, the too-textured world:
cratered pocks and scars of
the battered doorknob in my palm;
sharp blush of hot water against
my thigh, the bath's steam disguising
limbs, uncertain as their own reflections;
      kiwi's animal rasp
      on my tongue;

skins which are not skin.

O daylight things,
      pull me from this desire
      which is not hunger

but a fist
      beating its one message
on glass:

There is no one I would not touch.

HOSPICE

The first time I was terrified
I would kill her,

that the tube of morphine
would do what a stroke

and five years of dementia could not:
so I waited too long, till

the grimaces were gone,
before giving her sleep.

The nurse berated me
later: *If she is in pain, you ease*

that pain. That is our only goal.
This is why

it is impossible
to be a good daughter:

I knew she would die
no matter what I did,

and still I ached for her
to live. Each night,

I begged the gods
for only one of us

to wake up.

STRENGTH

1.
At my age,

my mother, a black belt
in judo, could toss a man
twice her size over her shoulder,
like salt.

A woman can't forget
that kind of power.

2.
My brother says, *I hope she doesn't die.*
He looks at me from eyelids that once barely opened,

that other doctors wanted cut
and realigned, made wide

so we could be sure if he was sleeping.
My brother, whose IQ is half mine—

who asks if he will have a stroke, too—
thanks me when I tell him no,

as though I've done him a favor.
She'll close her eyes,

then nothing, he tells me.
We don't yet know

she's even lost the strength
to shut her eyes.

THINGS SHE'S FORGOTTEN

How to make coffee. What you do
after you open a car door.

Her street address.
To check the mail.

Her fear of cats. The names
of sons. Her wedding dress,

how much it cost.
Her college town and all

its streets, the books she kept.
The books she threw away.

Her tiny dog, named George.
Her mother's house. Her maiden name.

What she wanted.
What it is to want.

WAKING

The worst part of brain surgery
for you was the moment you woke
to find yourself bald:
because you could not remember
cause and effect,
your naked skull
shocked you pale.
Don't look at my hair
you said. We didn't.
We looked at the staples instead.

Anne Marie Rooney

Writing the Poem with My Breath

All I and what's inside. All I, and what's
become. When a grin breaks apart an open
new eye. Say, I have been hoping and waiting
to stop looking. I have been outside of
outside, of outside. The roots molded, too.
And the plant, what's become, real of ether.
I hid behind a glass empty. Hidden behind once
and walloped. Inside that ending a new one
rose up. Rise up, new starry world. New theater
of crickets blurring another night closed. Inside
the fell balloon mouths open and awe.
All I know falls out of pose.

ANNE MARIE ROONEY

Sincerely something is the crush of my heart
inside of where what is. It's said real bones
poke outwards, so the station goes out
into darkness like land mining true. You said
that hair was good, it stopped the air
from moving. I tape up a picture to see it: that picture
on the floor and glue peeling also. That fingers
spackle the been-stuck is clear, then cloudy; that a blush
inside a closet is nearly too happy is fact—and flashed light
across it. Behind me every window is bleating.

All of my little hands in all of the floors that they are.

All of the centers of groveling forward.

All of the kindnesses unmeant in time.

Always I am menial, rekempt. I carve out thinner spaces and minute.

Smally moving closer though to pillar I finite the library, block it downwards and true.

All of the lamps that I am.

All of the closing and having-blown-back.

A light comes through to deposit, it's round. It is flat on my window, it is round.

I feel the day slant coldly. Warmth depletes its spackles against some glass.

Little hands and little mountain of steam: blown-back.

And a drug and a drug and a drug.

Oh graceful, oh barren
groping. Hapless and twitch
of bird *clod clod clod* along the roof.
This wrong animal, this
pillow I use to smother
good sense. Twitch of sky, cloudwords,
and twitch of clubby
clicking heels. If heat seals
crooked skin what tape dregs up
is softer. An animal is ruined
in leather, leather in weather, but I
break rank, offer,
hobble dryly to the next glum
stick-em-up. Say I'm all ready, stuck-up,
oh named one, oh
granted wish for many, then get me
to a cobbler, a new
stoned hobby, a way better
to maroon my own missed
stitches. Blue grows, sickness
grows, and every slither therein
a crass heckle. This blanket was ripped
from this animal, from its skin and drek.
Cloth as a closeted sound, a mar
sloping bellwards.
In that wrapping hell
spins faster, lukewarming.
I have been sad, and this

Grateful that I am and proud of eve

Proud of what center I enter when entering becomes uneaten

And furnished

Grift of water ended sideways

A daughter I am inside of, who I make

I bike a million times past the dead animal

Still dead, who I am

I bike and become a sort of rot also

Grace in what bent realm

I am a borrowed turkey become badder stitched

My every sticker grown fallow on the bedroom floor

I, stickler for innocence

For keeping animals dead, my knees so closed, so closed

In black divots of sound tire popping

A hiss and popped fruit exploded in me centuries

When I am so closed that no music in me backpedals

When is that animal so dead

I made a book like a rock you could slide down.
To oil an animal closer to death.
Further.
In earth, which is black mud.
Of course I move darkly.
Creep book, infinity book.
Word at the river of night.
And black mud book.
Stars or bells on water moved across.
Slick of spilled night.
Where is the separateness.
My book was riding
Across.
So what is the center.
The staple. Heat of the moment
on noon and thus.
A little groveling, mouth noise.
I step closer to the frayed back needle.
Become so vast, so vast.
Then I stopped writing the poem with my breath.

I guess I am little girl tired like a log

My whole vision the vision, as if relaxed I am
spectacular

I want always to drink warm water in a cool room
or cool water

In a warm room I am erased by pleasure

My whole body the body I will chase until steepled

Until on the pillow a head goes down

It is not my head, it is only
my heart

Going down into sound into aching inside silver

I brush the cat when I feel
a crumpled person

The bell of darkness overcomes me

Going out

ARISA WHITE

TOUCHED BY BEAUTY

PAW

One of a million women on many buses to PA,
I'm new meat. She's a college senior. Alpha stagger
assesses if this is a piece to be tossed or left—
if I can last the short-fast road between her paws.

She sets back the pack, brushes her curls
from her eyes. I believe my childhood cat
taught me to receive her, how to welcome
her after the previous smiles have failed.

I cannot take on her sorrow's torch;
it withers bright before a drowning heart,
beneath a roofless stare—she wants me to stay.

My eyes travel Philly's curbs,
enter the rust and tongueless Liberty Bell,
loop then double constrict her wrists,
and we agree, *bananas* for safety.

STRANGERS

Dark as being at the bottom of a well,
may beetles fall on us and the closed gas station.
Once a waterbug hung from my headscarf.
It was the touch of someone coming from behind.
We're lost in Texas. Hit a dead deer and lost the wheel
on our trailer. Sorry you left your camp gear
on the roadside. I forgot to say thank you; I was afraid.
We're queer and you look too much boy and good thinking
taking the rainbow off the plates in Maryland—
no one looked at us longer than needed.
Now we're at the point where we can't wake
ourselves out of it. We didn't start out on backroads—
on Route 116 in a college town, I whispered
I want to hang from her wallet chain.
You heard, stopped at the path's end.
I approached but this dark is not your smile.
Your chain is noise in a Texan's sleep. You step
into the light to pick up a signal, the least distracted
by beetles, and the wish being made on us tonight.

GLASS

Glass eye, glass heart, glass jar, in which we try and keep our flickering selves,
all the light in us is sexual, a luminous persistence—a heaven or a hell.
                                        - Rebecca Seiferle

Carved Susie in a banana skirt, sea dollar and winded instruments
collected in my pockets; Bach-dressed monkeys, tagged and used for study;
and the terrible feeling of someone betraying the way I stay preserved.

Discovered at three: a broom's bristle touch behind Easter dresses.
I'm without guilt. No need for truth or dare, dare or truth has no strings on me—
each one of us are souvenir globes, still or disturb, sand and coladas of a vacation.

The problem with returning ex-girlfriends—their hands elsewhere.
To redeem herself, she comes like a hound, turns to watch my rage
brandish its mane. Before orgasm, before we're sentinels with tears—

No uncle, no cry in a room full of she and I.
Adulterous berry, sweet and so winter, writes her name,
a heart, then the first letter we learn—a weak epoxy's promise.

I direct her to lovers who are amenable, who'll afghan
on ice-queen nights and stroke along her grain.
I do this than admit the cracks through me.

TOO MUCH TIME IN THE ROUGH

If you think you got the prize, there must
be an additional puff in your chest.

There must be deference for the means
by which I came, for all before.

There must be a hearty thank you
that makes the congregation whoop in accord.

Truly your shoulders are dusted—
you don't think highly of the one I left.

I will always be her "precious jewels"—
everyone else loses shine.

You spend too much time in the rough,
each gesture sets off waves and you came

from an impulse I've caged, and I regret
I cannot be both our wings.

You don't understand my ladders—the need
to be spotted and what if I'm a zebra?

CLOSET CASE

It's not hard to hold you, your cries
have shaken you, you seem freezing.
You've beaten the dog, her eyes are red,
hidden behind your guitar and frightened to bark.
You threaten to throw yourself from the ledge—
who will catch you?

No people on this sidewalk,
they're inside watching news, eating
Spanish food from the Spanish Restaurant.
Whoever's out will regard your flight
like the first sign of rain—
speed up and try to find an awning before it storms.

> *you shout you are stupid, look to accuse me*
> *of sharing the belief, no, stupid, you are not—yes,*
> *i am stupid. no those things, you should not say.*

We are lovers. When climbing the last five steps,
screams from behind your locked door serrates.
Someone is beating you, robbing boxes of books,
your wallet you can never find. You're on your knees,
tugging your hair—snap your neck from your clavicle
then this room will hear my lullaby.

You I cannot wake in morning
spent the night carving your own sunrise.
Red circle and rays of pink pucker,
your throat buckled your breath
when you saw it run to the carpet.
The towel was not enough bandage.
My fingers pressed on each line, afloat like carrion—
sticks and rotten bark that becomes of a failed escape.

You bled not to take you to the hospital.

> *i'm fucked up you shout, look to accuse the*
> *belief of sharing me. not fucked up, no you are.*
> *yes, so fucked I am. say those things, you shouldn't.*

The next time I will watch you,
clean the razor. Handcuff my hands to your wrists.
Breasts to back will pulse our sweat. Next time
your hands crave to cut—my fingers with the blade.

PRAY FOR SIGNS YOU DON'T READ

Last time a lighter was thrown
toward your face, it burned.

You're hit in the head.
Pray for signs you don't read.

You're waiting for the day you don't ruin,
not the dame who said she saw you in a dream—

all those pedestals bring out masochistic you.
Folsom Street Fair with your balls in a knot.

Whipped then whispered to while the lash settles.
You're pleasured by that butterfly hitting the skylight

and the keeper who says, Why do you keep doing this?
Never you say it's in your nature.

Now you understand her gentleness, her care
to allow you to struggle from your walls.

You were touched by beauty and injured.

CRAVES

The words might as well be bar coasters,
mess in pockets detergent don't clean.
I encounter in myself an end.

What to do with empty legs, stillness
that consents to punishment?
I've been reckless.

You reveal undone seams after another,
your pain a burden of worms,
looking for unstormed ground.

I watch you like porn, pleasured
and disgusted by how much you wanted it.
Believed marriage would make us better.

I know this saga as my mother's daughter;
it's nice to paw a mouse
until its guts spill—I need to retract.

You weathery over not getting
the hand-me-down way I love,
means your heart is unconditional.

Me not wanting to give
the hand-me-down way I love
means I'm sorry.

Like your mother's shot glasses,
there are things that distract
you from your abandonment—

I love the smell of mothballs

for the memory of my grandmother,
but it's her daughter who's in my closets.

LADY IN THE BOAT

I'm here, beautifully unadorned, my words pears.
I know your gardens, her bent-over back, her knees
in this earth, our mother's hands.

I've been searching for one pure answer, one complete
thing to feed loss. Something grown for your mouths,
a recipe my pans don't refuse.

Laboring between the hard-between and not a break,
amiss in the atmosphere are mutated eves, we are
first-stage zombie.

We've put our purses on ground and when we dream
of fish, we don't want them pregnant. There is a snake
sucking your milk—and you like it.

When nails are painted red, it's a certain suggestion:
put on your feathers and make thunder with your plow.
I may be over-ripened.

Spoiled because I was left to go soft. Willing yourself
from under the weight of too little admiration—
ladybugs took up residence.

Roots get suffocated and need broader reach.
Mirrored as unseen or caricature of another, I
think what's wrong with me?

On top of the sheets, in my street clothes, oscillating
fan stopped in my direction, in your small paradise
tomatoes were city in taste.

The dirt so dry it was a dying kiss—love changes

your want. You went into the yard and brought back
the match of your devotion.

After 25 years underwater, the town resurfaces.
Its first breath startles the wound. The ruins
we left are born again.

I've been told to starve them but there's no need.
Saying thank you to an abandoned face has no
bearing on her now.

You're a bone in her voice she pitched a long time
ago. I have jade and regrets and when I'm held
in a dark place, this body sarcophagus.

The excavation happening around me, it's grief—
ancient and never born—turns me sour,
feels of little good.

I wonder about these honeycombs,
these elegant divides. We all know
it takes a village to raise and kill a child.

Call them pollutants, I have proof we can
make clouds. From the snake below, I predict
the stones we lay our papers down.

There is one road in; you must walk
through someone's living room to get out.
You're not standing alone, the radio tuned,

in your bedroom, to a yesteryear song. You are
affirmative in your dance, some forgotten
vocabulary dug from the deep

pockets of your purse, sweetly and august.

Through the crack I witness you.

Before I was ready to be seen, the fiend
saw me and then like that we shared
this object of me.

She wanted a means to her fix. A dollar
for seeing me switch my hips. Does this
desire for unconditional love inhale

into us the butcher's breath? We seek
what can never be mete, our appetites
requiring more traps and labor.

I'm at the bus stop rubbing my curves
down so they can fit less vulnerably.
Once in the woods I feel the multiplying

effect of one voice, frogs opening portals
beneath a Shandy night when moss
has a private touch.

I watch all my mother's hands to see
her capabilities, what she kneads into her care,
the seasonings dropped into fish stew.

What broth is worthy of her spoons?
What she cooks and what she loves
has nuanced mixologies.

At first the natives couldn't see the Columbus
ships, no language for what's before their eyes.
There are those hindsights for consideration.

You say, I knew it in my gut and the gut got
ignored and what is wounded and wise,
confident and sure gets locked in a basement,

gets walked on all fours, gets internalization.
So many monkeys on our backs, you don't see
us anymore.

Some small tiny bugs, not ants, ate a 2ft weed
to the dirt—imagine what they do to our babies?
The eggshells that remained

from breakfast, baking cakes, or deviled eggs,
Granny mixed into the potting soil, her mother-
in-laws grew sharp tongues.

Is anger a machine that eats the heart's lion,
leaves it in a cave to approximate in sheep's wool?

For every month of March,
regardless of how you orchestrate it,
a drumline that hurts.

I don't know what armories you constructed
for all those arms estranged from their torsos—
a sign that soon you enter

a town of those who cannot pass from here.
This is not the same box that promises a VCR,
instead offers old news and expired coupons

to entertain our surprise that we don't get
what we pay for, that fantasy is altered
by the road—

what is given can be taken as not intended,
and forgiveness is a master of arrangement.

Ashley Inguanta

Cover Artist

"There is nothing more powerful, to me, than a woman becoming. Here, a woman becomes with water. I am thankful to have been there."
- Ashley Inguanta on this issue's cover image

Ashley Inguanta has photographed book covers for authors like Darlin' Neal and Joe Kapitan, and her individual photos have appeared in publications like *Redivider* (where she was featured as a spotlight artist) and *make/shift*. Ashley is also the Art Director of *SmokeLong Quarterly*.

CONTRIBUTORS

ALYSIA ANGEL is a southern-bred Lakota, and a working class queer high femme. She is self-published in chapbooks entitled *what i do when you're not looking* and *Brace Yourself*, an Amazon e-book. She is also published in *Femme Family* zine, *Q Zine*, *Salacious Magazine*, *Hot & Heavy: Fierce Fat Girls on Life, Love & Fashion*, *Bay Woof Magazine*, *Cactus Heart Magazine*, *Curve Magazine*, *Say Please*, and *Leather Ever After*. Alysia is a 2011 and 2012 Lambda Literary Fellow. Her website is www.alysiaangel.com.

JESSICA RAE BERGAMINO lives in Seattle, where she is an MFA candidate at the University of Washington. Her work has appeared or is forthcoming in *Fourteen Hills*, *The Berkeley Poetry Review*, and *Mason's Road*, among others.

TAMIKO BEYER is the author of *We Come Elemental* (Alice James Books), winner of the 2011 Kinereth Gensler Award, and *bough breaks* (Meritage Press). In addition to writing poems about queer desire, water, and ecology, she also is the Associate Communications Director at the Boston-based watchdog organization, Corporate Accountability International, where she harnesses the written word to challenge some of the most powerful and abusive corporations in the world.

CONTRIBUTORS

SOSSITY CHIRICUZIO is an outlaw poet and writer, a working-class/poly/fat/bearded queer femme, and a sex radical body positive activist. Her work can be found in *The Second Coming, Bitch Goddess, Say Please, Leather Ever After, Salacious Magazine*, on her CD, *Hand to Mouth*, in her book, *Stir the Juice*, and most often on the stage at Dirty Queer.

CHERYL CLARKE is the author of four books of poetry, *Narratives: poems in the tradition of black women* (1982), *Living as a Lesbian* (1986), *Humid Pitch* (1989), *Experimental Love* (1993), the critical study, *After Mecca: Women Poets and the Black Arts Movement* (Rutgers Press, 2005), and *The Days of Good Looks: Prose and Poetry 1980-2005* (Carroll and Graf, 2006). She continues to write poetry and essays. She has written a chapbook entitled *By My Precise Haircut*. Though she has written many essays over the years relevant to the black queer community, "Lesbianism: an act of resistance," which first appeared in the iconic *This Bridge Called My Back: Writings By Radical Women of Color* (Anzaldua and Moraga, eds., 1982) and "The Failure to Transform: Homophobia in the Black Community," which was published in the equally iconic *Home Girls: A Black Feminist Anthology* (Smith, ed., 1984) continue to be favorites. She considers herself a scholar of Audre Lorde and continues to write about the impact of Lorde's work. She recently wrote an introduction to *G.R.I.T.S., An Anthology of Writing by Southern Black Lesbians* (Williams, ed., Media Arts Project, 2013). Her article, "By Its Absence: Literature and Social Justice Consciousness" will appear in *The Handbook of Social Justice* (Reisch, ed., Routledge, 2014). She received the Kessler Award from the Center for Lesbian and Gay Studies at the CUNY Graduate Center in 2013. She finally retired from Rutgers University in July of 2013 after 41 years of studying, teaching, and administration on the New Brunswick campus. She is co-owner with her partner of 22 years, Barbara Balliet, of Blenheim Hill Books in Hobart, the Book Village of the Catskills.

THERESA DAVIS is the mother of three and was a classroom teacher for over twenty years. She reclaimed her love for poetry ten years ago after the loss of her father. Since then, she has been a member of the ArtsInterface, Co-founder of Art Amok Slam Team, Women of the World Slam Champion (2011), poet in residence as the 2012 McEver Chair of Georgia Tech University, Emerging Artist Grant Recipient, co-producer of the staged poetry performance with Jon Goode "Wish You Were Here," and was honored by the City of Atlanta with a proclamation making May 22 Theresa Davis Day. In July 2012, Theresa released her chapbook, *Simon Says,* poems about teaching and anti-bullying. This project, in partnership with the City of Atlanta's Bureau of Cultural Affairs, is a call to action to bring about an end to bully culture in our children's classrooms. In May 2013, Theresa released her first full-length collection of poems entitled *After This We Go Dark* (Sibling Rivalry Press), which was honored by the American Library Association through inclusion on its Over the Rainbow list of recommended LGBT-focused publications. *After This We Go Dark* is now in libraries all across the world.

LEAH HORLICK is a writer from Saskatoon. A 2012 Lambda Literary Fellow in Poetry, her work has appeared in *So To Speak, Plenitude, Canadian Dimension, GRAIN, Poetry is Dead,* and on *Autostraddle.* Her first book, *Riot Lung* (Thistledown Press, 2012), was shortlisted for a Saskatchewan Book Award. Horlick lives in Vancouver where she co-curates the city's only queer and anti-oppressive reading series.

ASHLEY INGUANTA [Cover Artist] is a writer/photographer who recently moved to Brooklyn from Central Florida. Her first collection, *The Way Home,* is out with Dancing Girl Press (and has been re-published for Kindle with The Writing Disorder), and she has translated the collection into a live performance, too, with dancing and music. She's published writing in many journals including *PANK, The Doctor T.J. Eckleburg Review, Wigleaf, Gone Lawn,* and *Sweet: A Literary Confection.* This year, her poem "San Andreas Fault," which appears in *The Ampersand Review,* was nominated for the Pushcart Prize. Her new chapbook collection of poetry, *For The Woman Alone,* is forthcoming with Ampersand Books in Spring 2014.

LAURA PASSIN is writer, professor, and feminist at large. She holds a PhD from Northwestern and an MFA from the University of Oregon. Her poetry has recently appeared in *Prairie Schooner* and *Bellevue Literary Review,* and she is working on her first poetry manuscript, *Aphasia,* which deals with illness, grief, and the loss of language. She lives in Chicagoland with her partner, two cats, and way too many books.

ANNE MARIE ROONEY is the author of *Spitshine* (Carnegie Mellon University Press, 2012), as well as the chapbooks *The Buff* (The Cupboard,

2011) and *Shell of an egg in an effort* (Birds of Lace, 2013). Her work has been featured in *Best New Poets* and *Best American Poetry* anthologies. A founding member of Line Assembly, she currently lives in New Orleans, where she works as a teaching artist.

ARISA WHITE received her MFA from UMass, Amherst. She's a Cave Canem fellow and the author of *Post Pardon, Hurrah's Nest*, and *A Penny Saved*. Her debut collection, *Hurrah's Nest*, won the 2012 San Francisco Book Festival Award for poetry and was nominated for a 44th NAACP Image Award, the 82nd California Book Awards, and the 2013 Wheatley Book Awards. A 2013-14 recipient of an Investing in Artist Grant from the Center for Cultural Innovation and an advisory board member for Flying Object, Arisa is a BFA faculty member at Goddard College.

VALERIE WETLAUFER [Editor of *Adrienne*] is a poet, doula, editor, and teacher. She holds an MFA from Florida State University, and a PhD from the University of Utah. Her first full-length poetry collection *Mysterious Acts by My People* was published by Sibling Rivalry Press in March 2014. She lives in Iowa.

SUBMIT TO *ADRIENNE*

We encourage submissions to *ADRIENNE* by queer women poets of any age, regardless of background, education, or level of publication experience. For more information, visit us online at www.siblingrivalrypress.com.

CPSIA information can be obtained at www.ICGtesting.com
Printed in the USA
LVOW12s2048160414

382017LV00001B/1/P